TRADITIONAL SONGS

Clementine

Edited by Ann Owen
Illustrated by Sandra D'Antonio

Music Consultant: Peter Mercer-Taylor, Ph.D.,
Associate Professor of Musicology
University of Minnesota, Minneapolis, Minnesota

Reading Consultant: Susan Kesselring, M.A., Literacy Educator
Rosemount-Apple Valley-Eagan (Minnesota)
School District

PICTURE WINDOW BOOKS
MINNEAPOLIS, MINNESOTA

Traditional Songs series editor: Peggy Henrikson
Page production: The Design Lab
Musical arrangement: Elizabeth Temple
The illustrations in this book were rendered in pen with digital coloring.

PICTURE WINDOW BOOKS
5115 Excelsior Boulevard
Suite 232
Minneapolis, MN 55416
1-877-845-8392
www.picturewindowbooks.com

Printed in the United States of America.

Library of Congress Cataloging in Publication Data
Clementine / edited by Ann Owen ; illustrated by Sandra D'Antonio.
p. cm. — (Traditional songs)
Includes bibliographical references (p.).
ISBN 1-4048-0155-3 (hardcover)
ISBN 1-4048-0423-4 (softcover)
Summary: Presents an illustrated version of the traditional song along with some
discussion of its folk origins.
1. Folk songs, English—United States—History and criticism—Juvenile literature.
2. Children's songs—Texts. [1. Gold mines and mining—Songs and music. 2. Songs.]
I. Owen, Ann, 1953– II. D'Antonio, Sandra, 1956– ill. III. Series.
ML3551 .C53 2003
782.42162'13'00268—dc21
2002155277

What do you see when you sing a song? Does the music come in colors?

What do you do when you sing a song? Does the melody make you dance?

What do you hear when you sing a song? Do the words tell a story?

Let's explore the sights and sounds of one of our favorite songs.

Who is that girl with the strange looking shoes?

In a cavern, in a canyon,
excavating for a mine,

lived a miner, forty-niner,
and his daughter, Clementine.

Light she was
and like a fairy,
and her shoes
were number nine.

Herring boxes without topses,
sandals were for Clementine.

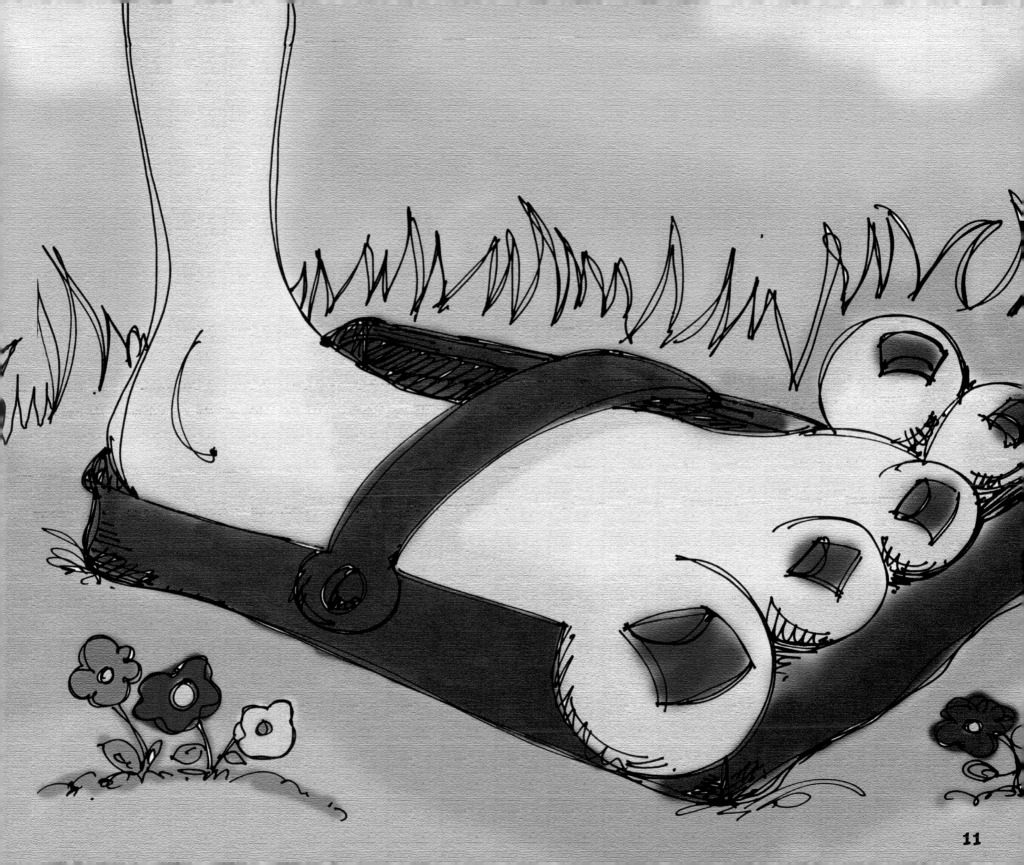

Drove her ducklings
to the water
ev'ry morning
just at nine.

Hit her foot against a splinter, fell into the foaming brine.

Ruby lips above the water,
blowing bubbles soft and fine.

But alas, I was no swimmer,
so I lost my Clementine.

Oh, my darling,
oh, my darling,
oh, my darling, Clementine!
You are lost and gone forever.
Dreadful sorry,
Clementine.

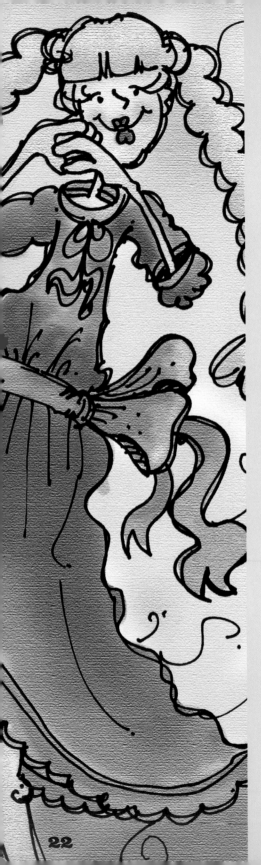

Clementine

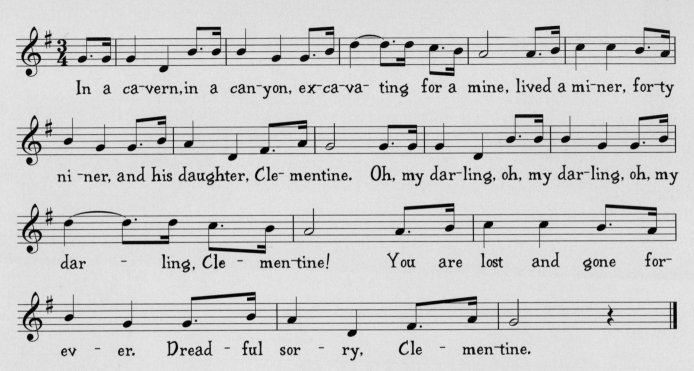

In a ca-vern, in a can-yon, ex-ca-va-ting for a mine, lived a mi-ner, for-ty ni-ner, and his daughter, Cle-mentine. Oh, my dar-ling, oh, my dar-ling, oh, my dar - ling, Cle - men-tine! You are lost and gone for- ev - er. Dread - ful sor - ry, Cle - men-tine.

2. Light she was and like a fairy,
And her shoes were number nine.
Herring boxes without topses,
Sandals were for Clementine.

CHORUS
Oh, my darling,
Oh, my darling,
Oh, my darling, Clementine!
You are lost and gone forever.
Dreadful sorry, Clementine.

3. Drove her ducklings to the water
Ev'ry morning just at nine.
Hit her foot against a splinter,
Fell into the foaming brine.

CHORUS
Oh, my darling,
Oh, my darling,
Oh, my darling, Clementine!
You are lost and gone forever.
Dreadful sorry, Clementine.

4. Ruby lips above the water,
Blowing bubbles soft and fine.
But alas, I was no swimmer,
So I lost my Clementine.

CHORUS
Oh, my darling,
Oh, my darling,
Oh, my darling, Clementine!
You are lost and gone forever.
Dreadful sorry, Clementine.

About the Song

Clementine's story came from the time of the California gold rush. Gold was found in California in the late 1840s. In 1849, about 80,000 people flocked to California to seek their fortunes. These gold-hunters were known as "forty-niners."

No one knows for sure who wrote the song "Clementine." Early versions of the song show that H.S. Thompson wrote the words. Then in the early 1880s, the words and music were published together. At that time, the poet Percy Montross was listed as the author. Most likely, "Clementine" was like many old songs and had no single author. Maybe it started when someone put a fun story or poem to a popular tune, then others kept adding or changing verses.

DID YOU KNOW?

Gold was most often found in tiny nuggets or gold dust. Sometimes, however, a large gold rock was uncovered. The largest gold rock ever found was discovered in Australia in 1872. "The Holtermann Nugget" weighed almost 639 pounds (290 kilograms). This is about the weight of three large men put together!

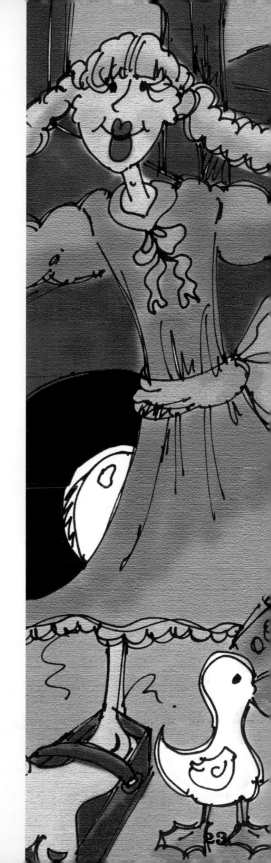

Make a Musical Instrument: Chimes

WHAT YOU NEED:

- ruler or dowel about the length of a ruler
- paint or markers
- ribbon
- 1 piece of string 18 inches (46 centimeters) long
- 5 (or more) pieces of string 7 inches (18 centimeters) long
- 5 (or more) washers or old keys or a combination of both
- paint or markers
- nail polish *
- metal spoon

WHAT TO DO:

1. Decorate the ruler or dowel by painting, coloring, and/or attaching ribbon streamers to the ends. Allow the paint to dry.
2. Tie one end of the long piece of string to one end of the ruler and the other end of the string to the other end of the ruler. This will give you a hanger for your chimes.
3. Hang the washers, keys, or both from the ruler (or dowel) with the short pieces of string. Space them out evenly. You may choose to hang them at different lengths.
4. Play your chimes by striking the washers or keys with a metal spoon.

* You can make your chimes colorful by painting the washers or keys first with different color nail polishes, such as red, gold, glittery, etc. The polish sticks well to the metal, but be sure to have an adult help you!

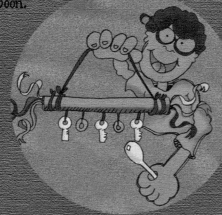

To Learn More

AT THE LIBRARY

Altman, Linda Jacobs. *The Legend of Freedom Hill.* New York: Lee & Low Books, 2000.

Coerr, Eleanor. *Chang's Paper Pony.* New York: Harper & Row, 1988.

Kay, Verla. *Gold Fever.* New York: Putnam's, 1999.

Krull, Kathleen. *Gonna Sing My Head Off!: American Folksongs for Children.* New York: A.A. Knopf, 1992.

Roop, Peter and Connie. *California Gold Rush.* New York: Scholastic Reference, 2002.

ON THE WEB

CHILDREN'S MUSIC WEB
http://www.childrensmusic.org
For resources and links on children's music for kids, parents, educators, and musicians

NATIONAL INSTITUTE OF ENVIRONMENTAL HEALTH SCIENCES KIDS' PAGES: CHILDREN'S SING-ALONG SONGS
http://www.niehs.nih.gov/kids/musicchild.htm
For music and lyrics to many favorite, traditional children's songs

FACT HOUND
Want more information about traditional songs? FACT HOUND offers a safe, fun way to find Web sites. All of the sites on Fact Hound have been researched by our staff. Simply follow these steps:

1. Visit *http://www.facthound.com.*
2. Enter a search word or 1404801553.
3. Click Fetch It.

Your trusty Fact Hound will fetch the best sites for you!